LAY PREACHERS

IN THE

CHURCH OF ENGLAND;

OR,

A PRACTICAL PROPOSAL TO REACH THE SPIRITUALLY DESTITUTE IN THICKLY POPULATED PARISHES.

RESPECTFULLY DEDICATED TO THE

BISHOPS & CLERGY OF THE CHURCH OF ENGLAND.

LONDON: SIMPKIN, MARSHALL, & Co.

LICHFIELD: EGGINGTON & BROWN.

PRICE THREEPENCE.

PREFACE.

"In town parishes the great want is living agents, who, by the personal influence of their own holiness of life and conversation, may induce the masses to listen to the teaching of religion, and bring them within reach of the means of grace. It is in this that the work of Sisters and Deaconessess has been so blessed. A solution of the difficulty might possibly be found in making the Diaconate a permanent Order in the Church, instead of its remaining little more than a stepping-stone to the Priesthood. If there were Deacons permitted to discharge the Clerical functions appertaining to their Order, and at the same time occupied in some secular work on which they chiefly depended for their maintenance, the Church might have many useful assistants added to her ranks without any great additional strain upon her finances."—ADDITIONAL CURATES' REPORT, 1875.

The above important extract, combined with a deep impression of the value of tens of thousands of perishing souls and the inability of the present provision of clergy to preach the word of life to those souls, led the Author to resolve to make some humble effort to suggest a remedy. And if anything can give him confidence in the success, under God, of his proposed plan, it is the fact that the main suggestions advanced, as to the raising and working of Lay Preachers, are not theories, but have been tried with good and great results.

The Author lays no claim to perfection in his proposed scheme. His desire is to offer his contribution to solve a problem which, to every reflective mind, must present issues that are awfully momentous. It it also hoped that with the carrying out of the scheme, many a godly and earnest Churchman, though not a Lay Preacher, will find openings for Christian labour where but little or nothing of the kind at present exists. It has been a complaint with some that in the Church of England they do not find facilities for the use of their talents such as are afforded amongst Nonconformists. We recently received a letter from an intelligent, earnest, and rising member amongst a section of the Nonconformists, who attributes his leaving the Church, a short time since, to the fact that in his parish (thickly populated) he had no opportunity to use his talents. With fields white unto harvest, and with so few labourers, God forbid that any hindrance should be put in the way of those who are willing, within proper bounds, to do what they can to save souls. If we mistake not, there is a growing wish on the part of the earnest, intelligent laity, to more heartily engage, than formerly, in doing what they can to extend the kingdom of Christ in the world. And we are abundantly glad that, in connection with this feeling, many of the most devoted clergy are shewing their sympathy, and so, in the language of the Primate, in one of his recent Visitations, are "keeping abreast of the times." May He "for whom are all things and by whom are all things" give to every good plan His abundant blessing.

Postscript. To obtain suggestions for the improvement of his scheme, the Author sent out about fifty interleaved copies. The result has been very cheering. Bishops, parish clergymen, nobles, &c , have alike welcomed the following pages and given valuable suggestions. The suggestions sent in have been of a four-fold order, viz :—1. Two or three would sacrifice everything to their Shibboleths. The Shibboleth of the Author has been to surrender some of his conservative opinions, so as to make an attempt to save souls. 2. Some suggestions (especially one noble lord's) have been so extended as to make it impracticable to insert all of them. If possible, the remainder will appear in a future edition. 3. Two would lessen, in some pages, the details. But as several of the most practicable and legislative correspondents have thought otherwise, the details are retained. Still, let it be borne in mind that the pamphlet throughout is not made up of hard and fast lines, but is a series of special *proposals* to meet special needs—such proposals being designed to suggest some practical outlines of action. 4. Some, including W. E. Gladstone, M.P., Lord Selborne, &c., have approved of the principle, providing all can be kept under proper authority. Without being invidious, the Author tenders his most sincere thanks to all who have kindly aided him, and he will feel very grateful to any of his readers who will favour him with any facts, emendations, etc. That he might as far as possible, make his effort universally acceptable, the Author has had suggestions for every school of thought in the Church, and such have been, more or less, accepted.

Address :—Author, St. George's, Wolverhampton.

CONTENTS

LAY PREACHERS

I. *The Definition of a Lay Preacher.*

A Lay Preacher shall be understood to be a man who holds a license from a Bishop to preach in a given parish, subject to the direction of the Incumbent of such a parish. Further, he shall follow his regular worldly calling on week days, and give his labours gratuitously on Sundays, or at other leisure times. This, however, shall not be so interpreted as to preclude the possibility of making an arrangement for giving a salary to any man who may be hired for special and consecutive mission work, which shall include preaching. This, done very frequently amongst Nonconformists, is, we believe, already carried out in a few parishes. For further particulars, as to his position in the parish, and his relationship to his Incumbent, &c., see Chap. XIII. and XV.

II. *A Defence of Lay Preaching.*

The remarks of this chapter will only briefly deal with the general question. For answers to several particular objections, see Chap. XVIII.

Passing over the preachers of the Old Testament, who, although prophetical, were in most instances outside of the priestly tribe, we think we discern an order of Lay Preachers in the seventy disciples. But whether so, or not, "lay presbyters" appear to have exerted some influence in the Christian Church at the close of the second century. And this may account for the opinion of some that Justin Martyr (A.D. 150) was a Lay Preacher. About A.D. 215, Origen was appointed a Lay Preacher in the Church by Theoctistus Bishop of Cæsarea (Palestine), and by Alexander, Bishop of Jerusalem. Either one, or both, being expostulated with by Demetrius, Bishop of Alexandria, the reply was a reference to special cases for such a practice, *e. g.*, Euelpis, Paulinus, and Theodorus being appointed by their respective Bishops. (Bingham Antiq., Bk. 14, cp. 4, § 4.) The 4th Coun. of Carthage (A.D. 398) permitted lay men to teach, if so requested by the clergy. And if permitted to press into our service an illustration from the Papal church we would remark that at the 4th Lateran Council (A.D. 1215), permission was given to establish an order of Lay Preachers, known as the Order of Dominican Friars. That their moral tone did not equal their zeal does not invalidate the worth of our argument. To come down to later times: —At a most important discussion of the York Convocation of 1865, on lay preaching, several speakers evidenced a feeling in favour of persons being licensed as Lay Preachers. One or two bore valuable testimony to the power for good of lay preaching amongst the Wesleyans, and the Bishop of Durham said that he would gladly give a license for preaching to any proper lay man who asked him for it. The license spoken of did not imply liberty to preach in consecrated buildings, but in such places as were found suitable, whether licensed or unlicensed. And our proposed plan does not contemplate lay preaching in parish churches, though, in the opinion of the Bishop of Lincoln, it is doubtful whether it is forbidden by law. (See Irenicum Wesleyanum. *Lincoln, Williamson.*) In support of his views, he refers to Bingham's Antiquities, the Canons of 1603 (Canon 36) and the Act of Uniformity Amendment Act of 1872. A most valuable paper in favour of lay preaching (see *Guardian*, Nov. 1, 1876) was read at the Diocesan Conference of Lincoln (October, 1876), by Chancellor Benson, and a resolution was passed approving of the same. But whilst judging from lay preaching in ancient times, and also from the foregoing, that a special case might be made out in favour of lay preaching in regular Churches, our aim is to reach those outside the church, who do not, and will not, go to church, nor chapel, and consequently must be reached through other channels. In view, then, of the foregoing, and remembering that in many churches lay readers are employed, and that here and there may be found men of high social position and great moral worth who hold licenses from their respective Bishops to preach the Gospel, there can be no reasonable condemnation of lay preaching, as a general principle.

III. *A Plea for Lay Preaching.*

Were we disposed, we might do very much to substantiate our plea by taking some such ground as follows: —A National Church to be truly national ought so to make provision that all who compose the nation should hear the Gospel. What is true of a National Church, is true of a Parish Church. But if it can be proved that in a nation there are several millions, and in a parish several thousands, who, with the existing agency, cannot have the word of life preached to them, the appellations "national church" and "parish church" are very inappropriate, nay, the church is in a very deficient state and stands in need of some other helping agency. Does such a deficiency of provision exist? The answer must be in the affirmative. Not to mention the aggregate numbers of tens of thousands in our large cities (e. g. Manchester and Birmingham), and hundreds of thousands in London who are almost, if not altogether ignorant of the existence of the Second Person in the Trinity, we come to parishes. With some care in the matter, the Author has, in reference to those who attend no place of worship, arrived at alarming results. Hundreds of parishes are correctly represented as follows :—" Out of 15,000 in my parish, 9000 attend no place of worship ;" " there are in my parish 10,000, above 6000," &c. ; " Out of 9000, at least 5000," &c. In many of those parishes the clerical staff is only two ("V. and C."). And in very few indeed does the staff go beyond three in number. But even in some parishes where the staff is an incumbent and three curates, it is impossible to do more than reach the outskirts of the masses. We could mention incumbents who, with their curates, are incessantly at work and yet who, with the consciousness of making such little impression on the kingdom of Satan around them, are sunk, at times, into a half despondent state. A letter bearing on the subject is now before us. The parish is large ; the vicar and his two curates are incessantly at work (" work, work, nothing but work "), 5000 out of 9000 are almost practically home heathens ; but so utterly unable is the devoted minister, with his present staff, to cope with the abounding indifference, that, at times, he is half tempted to give up all in despair.

Here then is an appalling picture ; a terrible fact,—thousands of one's own neighbours perishing for the bread of life, and no one to take it to them. What can be done to meet the sadly existing need? The periodical " Mission " which is held with so much benefit in many parishes, is an attempt, but only a very imperfect one, to meet the case. Still is the question asked, What can be done? The Author's answer is, secure, in each of the foregoing parishes, a band of devoted Lay Preachers. Such agents are the very backbone of several sections of the Nonconformists, and if to them so important, why not be of great value in the Church of England? That the reader may see the paramount importance of "Local Preachers" amongst the Methodists, we will give an illustration from a respectable "circuit" in the West of England. The number of ministers on the circuit is four; the number of Local Preachers about 30; the number of Chapels 20; the number of hearers in those chapels is about 6000; the number of sermons in each chapel on Sunday is two; and the number of week-night sermons will average, in each chapel, three per month; (total average, per week, 55 sermons). A moment's reflection on the machinery of this circuit before us (a fair sample to illustrate the value of lay agency in about 1500 others) must convince the most sceptical that our plea for Lay Preachers is not based upon a mere theory, and that, without such aid, Nonconformist ministers could not possibly keep going their ever-active machinery. We have heard some say, "Increase the number of Curates," or "Let the Church give better stipends to the Curates, and there will be a larger supply of candidates for Holy Orders, and so there will be no necessity for Lay Preachers." Something may be said in favour of such statements, but what if no curates and money are forthcoming? The Pastoral Aid Society does not appear sanguine about reaching all the masses through clerical agency, and it is well known that, with all special means in the shape of funds, Theological Colleges, &c., the supply of curates only just provides for the general wear and tear of the Church. It is well known that the increase of curates has not for a long time kept pace, by far, with the increase of population. It may be that in the course of future years more may be done than at present, but in the mean while what of thousands of dying souls in a vast multitude of parishes? We reply with emphasis, as quickly as possible, commence to train promising young men for Lay Preachers. We do not say that Lay Preachers will meet all the crying and increasing needs of the outside masses of the Church of England, but we have strong faith that they will do much towards it. And surely if Nonconformists can do so much, the Church of England, with all her better forces, ought to do a thousand fold more,

We see nothing else, at present, to supply the serious deficiency but Lay Preachers. and we believe that, with their co-operation, the complaint of certain would-be-monastic orders about the parochial system being a failure, would cease to be anything but a portion of "Old wives' tables."

IV. *An Essential on the part of the Incumbent in his attempt to raise up Lay Preachers.*

Let it ever be borne in mind that even one soul is worth saving, but how much more many souls? The most glorious work which can engage all the powers of man, and, if possible, create envy amongst angels is the effort to save souls. To succeed in this effort, there is one imperative qualification essential, and that is a burning love for souls. The souls of all their parishioners must be viewed as redeemed with the precious blood of Christ, as, in most cases, brought under the covenant of grace by baptism, and as, with all those privileges, being in danger of eternal death. Further, they must look upon themselves as shepherds of those souls, shepherds from whom, at the last day, the Redeemer and Judge will require an account of what has been done to save the souls in charge. In connection also with this view of the sacred office, there should be a study of Christ's weeping over Jerusalem, a vivid realization of what is implied in a heaven of eternal joy, and a hell of eternal misery, an abiding conviction that it is possible to belong to the unfaithful shepherds and watchmen of Ezekiel (Ezek. 33, 34.), and also a feeling that after all a minister may at last "become a cast-a-way." Unless the foregoing enter into an Incumbent's feelings there is no hope of real success. We cannot emphasize this point too strongly. Every future step will depend upon this first one. And in proportion to the intensity of the above feelings will be, humanly speaking, the measure of success. There may be on the part of the Incumbent an absence of superior, natural tact, or of very great abilities for enterprise, but let him have an unquenchable love for perishing souls, and he will have a power that will very much compensate for a lack of superior gifts. Grace is almighty. Let the Incumbent feel that the Holy Ghost is the purchased inheritance of the Church, let him feel that not only is the " power from on high " purchased to comfort and to sanctify the Church, but is purchased to convert the world, and let him earnestly seek and constantly depend upon His living and abiding presence in all his efforts, and he will get God's pledge of many and great blessings.

V. *The Incumbent breaking up fallow ground, &c.*

It is assumed that there is material in the parish. This assumed, the first effort should be a series of special sermons, (the announcement of the design of such sermons could be left to the decision of the Incumbent) beginning with personal consecration to God. (Probably a most opportune time for commencing the effort would be in connection with the " Mission," if one should be held). Suitable texts would be, " Choose you this day," &c. (Jos. xxiv. 15.) ; " Who is on the Lord's side ?" (Ezekiel xxxii. 26) ; " He that is not with me," &c. (Matt. xii. 30) ; " Now is the accepted time," &c (2 Cor. vi. 2) ; " Be not deceived, God is not mocked," &c. (Gal. vi. 7). Many others will suggest themselves. Having got a surrender of the soul, there must be a call to labour for Christ. Suitable texts are, "So teach us to number our days," &c. (Ps. xc. 12) ; " Go work in my vineyard" (Mat. xx. 4) ; " Whatsoever thy hand findeth to do," &c. (Ecc. ix. 10) ; " Curse ye Meroz," &c. (Jud. v. 23) ; " Lord, what wilt thou have me to do ?" (Acts ix. 7) ; The man with the one talent who was punished for not using it ; " Who gave Himself for us," &c. (Titus ii. 14) ; " Well done," &c. (Matt. xxv. 21.) At the close of each sermon, let there be a personal, solemn appeal for immediate decision for Christ and for Christian work. Intercourse, personally, or by letter, should be solicited. Let every one feel that the preacher will be glad to see any one who is willing to work for the Lord. Let this be done, and let any other special means be used until there is an earnest enquiry on the part of many, or several, about working for Christ.

VI. *Preliminary training of Christ's Voluntary Workers.*

Say, as a beginning, one has secured—eight, ten or twelve. Now, there must be an arrangement for at least one meeting each week, so as to talk to them in general, and to elicit from them answers to *simple* questions relative to Christian duties and doctrines. Let every meeting be connected with prayer and singing, and be sure to get two or three to pray at each meeting. No matter how short or how simple the prayer is—it will be a *beginning*. Should there be any particular case in the class, seek a private interview. The questions may be founded on the Bible or on the Prayer-Book. In all those meetings there must be kept alive the impression that life is uncertain, time is short, much has to be done, and God will hold all responsible for the use of gifts and privileges. As soon as possible, set them to work, by holding prayer-meetings in cottages, or rooms of some kind. Let as many, of the ten or twelve attend as is possible. Two at least should always be present. The cottage meeting should be lively in singing and short in prayers, intermingled with one or two short addresses. (This has frequently been tried with great success). Let there be two or three of those meetings every week, and let each meeting, if possible, be held in a separate place. But whilst doing this, let the places be so arranged as to work thoroughly a given district. Having got one company of workers, seek to secure another company, and so on, until there is enclosed, as in a spiritual net, the whole of the parish. That there be no confusion, a plan of places, and the companies to work them, should be prepared and strictly adhered to. As a rule, the plan should have to do with *week-day* meetings. On Sundays, say an hour before evening service, there should be a sort of general, or united prayer-meeting. Let this meeting be open to all. Such an arrangement would not only promote sympathy amongst the several companies, but would very much cheer the Incumbent's heart. If the prayers of the righteous are what the Bible represents them to be, how believingly, and so effectively, can the minister throw himself into the whole of the service, and especially into his pulpit ministrations. In all prayer-meetings, let the salvation of souls be kept in view. This must be done, not only by the person engaged in prayer, but by all in the meeting. Silently and expectingly, each one should be looking to heaven for a present blessing. We deem meetings for prayer as one of the best preparations to create sympathy for souls and to prepare a Lay Preacher for the sincere and energetic use of his talents. Ability to preach should, in some measure, be combined with ability to pray.

VII. *Further steps and preparatory training completed.*

First step:—In addition to the above prayer-meetings

for the cultivation and exercise of gifts, there must be, as a permanent institution, some kind of Bible, or Semi-Theological Class. This should be held weekly, and be presided over by the Incumbent, or his Curate. The subjects brought before the class and the mode of treating the same must be left to the judgement of the president and must depend upon the intellectual powers or attainments of the members. Out of two or three plans, the Author has found that the one which has been most successful (average attendance about 30) was to give each member a question on the next week's subject and expect him to do his best to answer it. It is desirable to get each member to give an oral answer. This, as may be naturally supposed, will be a most valuable exercise. Let each meeting of the class be connected with one or more short prayers by members of the class. By this means, and by the answers to the questions, the president will be able to form an approximate estimate of the intellectual and spiritual state of each member, and, also, who are the most promising for employment as Lay Preachers.

Second step :—This is a most important and critical one and must decide the value of all prior efforts. Upon a wise selection will depend all future success. And this selection cannot be too earnestly prayed about. The choice made and the chosen ones having given consent, special efforts must be made accordingly. First, they must be joined into a select class for theological training. And, secondly, they should, either from a text chosen by the Incumbent, or one chosen by themselves, prepare and read a short sermon before the class, and each member should be at liberty to kindly criticise both the manner of reading and the matter read. This the Author has found to be of immense service in many cases. An occasional discussion on a given doctrinal subject should, by all means, form a portion of the programme. An opportunity will thus be afforded for laying under contribution the Bible, the Prayer-Book, and standard works on theology. Many other topics will suggest themselves, such as What is the best kind of preaching? How shall we most successfully win souls for Christ? &c., &c. In the meanwhile, rooms should be secured for lay preaching, and, when the members are ready, the work should commence in earnest. It should be borne in mind that the preparatory and the select classes must be considered as permanent institutions. Removals by providential circumstances and (it is to be hoped) some seeking admission for Holy Orders will shew the propriety of this. As the Lay Preacher may find it of immense service in his after work, he should be encouraged to speak at the select class on a text chosen at the time, which to understand and arrange, a few minutes should be allowed. Thus far, briefly but we hope intelligently, we have glanced at the mode of preparation of men for Lay Preachers. An Incumbent may think that the whole involves a great deal of labour and anxiety. Yes, in some sense correct, but he should remember that, throughout the world, above 65,000 Lay Preachers, preaching the great fundamental truths of Christianity (*i.e.,* man's ruin, redemption, and recovery) have undergone similar training, directly or indirectly, at the hands of Nonconformist ministers. Surely the Church of England, in its 15,000 parishes, with its 23,000 clergy, need not be outstripped by the zeal and tact of those without her pale. With this digression, it is assumed that, in the opinion of the Incumbent, a certain person is fit to be recommended for examination, preparatory to receiving a license, and, as such, his Incumbent is prepared to recommend him.

VIII. *As to Examination and License.*

Some who are prepared to accept the principle of lay preaching, have expressed their fears about the possibility of having, as Lay Preachers, a large mixture of ignorant men. As a preventive of this, and in addition to the aforementioned preparatory training, there should be a formal examination. The examiners should at least comprise three. These might be the Rural Dean, the Lay Preacher's Incumbent, and some neighbouring Incumbent whom the Lay Preacher's Incumbent might choose. This would be a safe-guard, and is commendable for its simplicity.

The nature of the examinations:--1. A brief account of *why* he desires to be received as a Lay Preacher. 2. A *vivâ voce* examination on the Scripture proofs for the doctrines taught in the Apostle's Creed, the Nicene Creed, Athanasian Creed, and Articles 1, 2, 4, 5, 6, 9, 10, 11, 12, 13, 14, 15, 16, 18, 25, 27, 28, 31.* 3. A short, written sermon.

Perhaps it is desirable that each candidate for examination

---

* Some advise *all* the Articles. Let it be so if desired.

should state that he has read, say Paley's Evidences of Christianity, Humphrey on the Prayer-Book, Trollope on the Articles, and if possible, Smith on the O. and N. T. (These are mentioned because of size and price, and as containing much valuable matter in a popular form. However, others, of greater worth, may suggest themselves). He should also be required to give a formal assent to the Prayer Book and the Articles, as far as he understands them.

Providing the Examiners approve of the candidate, and so recommend to the Bishop, a license shall be issued forthwith. Some may suggest that the elements of grammar should form a part of the examination, and others may suggest that the Bishop should personally examine before he issued the license. The question of grammar, perhaps, had better be left with the Incumbent. As to the personal examination by the Bishop, it is more than probable that many would shrink from such an examination. Besides, in many dioceses such an examination would involve much extra labour for the Bishop. We would, therefore, suggest that the examination should be left in the hands of the aforesaid.

IX. *As to Preaching Places.*

The Lay Preacher being ready, the question is, Where shall he preach? As a general remark, we say get the best accommodation possible. If possible, get the aid of the well-to-do parishioners towards building and fitting up or hiring suitable places. In choosing sites for buildings, it is most desirable to keep in view the best centres. The quality and size of the Incumbent's preaching places must depend upon the demands and means. In the event of getting, or rearing a new one, the plans, &c. of the Incorporated Church Building Society (*Vide Church Builder,* April and July, 1875) should be consulted. According to its statement, " hamlet chapels " can be reared and supplied with all suitable furniture at £2 per head for each adult. But if no present means offer themselves for the securing of everything suitable, rather than be thwarted in carrying out plans, get the loan of workshops, &c. With seats of some kind, and a table or desk, such places (as have frequently been the case) may soon become the nucleus of a building and an audience, which shall be all that one could have expected. Though there be rooms, let there be no fear about *street preaching*. In some places, much of the residuum of the population may be most effectively reached by such means. Short, stirring addresses and lively singing have sometimes worked wonders. The street service concluded, one mode of attracting to the preaching room would be singing on the way. This practice, before a Sunday evening service, has been the means of doing much good. And by way of confirming the utility of such a mode of procedure, many parishes, in connection with their periodical "Mission," have adopted the principle with very much success.

As in many parishes there may not be found adequate means to get the most desirable preaching places, a very important question may be started, viz, the propriety of getting a Special Fund for such objects. This is done universally and with great effect amongst the Nonconformists A recent gift by one of them of £50,000 towards additional chapels shews, in this direction, a great amount of enthusiasm, and affords a fine example for imitation on the part of some princes of wealth in the Church of England. We need not remark that all of the Incumbent's important preaching places should be legally secured for the purposes for which they are intended. Besides being preaching places, they can be utilized for many other purposes, such as Sunday Schools, Lectures, Temperance Meetings, Week-night Prayer-meetings, &c. Every proper Preaching Place should, as soon as possible, be licensed by the Bishop for preaching and administering the Sacraments, and the holding of such services as, in the opinion of the Incumbent, shall conduce to the moral and spiritual welfare of his parishioners. In all cases, meetings, &c., held in the Preaching Places, shall have the sanction of the Incumbent. In connection with the making of provision for the administration of the Sacraments in the Preaching Places, let it always be understood to be a case of real necessity.

X. *As to the Nature of the Services, mode of conducting, length, &c.*

Whilst aware that we are supposed to handle a difficult subject and to tread upon debatable ground, much of both will pass away when the officiating person shall purely aim at saving souls, and shall strive to shew to his hearers that his one object is to point them to Christ and to fit them for heaven. When the Son of God taught the multitudes from a ship, beneath trees, and on mountain slopes, there need not be undue concern about a gorgeous ritual and an elaborate ceremonial. A heart full of love to perishing souls, and the tears of Jeremiah and the Psalmist, will very much compensate for the absence of many things that are deemed by some as all-important in religious worship. But whatever may, or may not be thought to be the requisite accessories of the worship of God, by all means let the service of the preaching room be simplicity itself. Local peculiarities or circumstances may be considered in the matter, but, as a rule, both morning and evening prayer should be shortened. In addition to the Psalms for the day, three or four good hymns, with lively and easy tunes should form a part of every service. The length of the sermon must be governed by circumstances. The subject treated, the talents of the preacher, &c., must very much rule in the matter. It would be better to divide the sermon by singing between, or have two persons to speak, than have a dull service. It has been strongly pressed upon us by a most successful lay worker and preacher of a large parish that the Sunday morning service should be exclusively for men. This, from the fact that it has worked with much success in the foregoing parish, is worthy of attention. The wives, in many neighbourhoods, appear to be forced to stay at home to cook the dinner. Get, however, the husbands and brothers to come, and wives and daughters will soon follow them, if not in the morning, they will in the evening. We say morning and evening, but in some places it is possible that *afternoon* and evening would be more suitable. In conclusion, there are two subjects which call for an observation. One is the mode of delivering the sermon and the other is the prayer-meeting at the conclusion of the evening service. If possible, it would be desirable for the Lay Preacher to avoid the use of manuscript. Reading sermons is scarcely known amongst the Local Preachers of Nonconformity. Still, rather than there be no sermon, or the sermon a mere string of repetitions, delivered with hesitancy and other defects, it is better to read. Good practical matter, earnestly and well read, will not fail to do good. Concerning the prayer-meetings, perhaps it is as well, on *winter* evenings, to make it a general rule to hold them. In many churches they are regularly held, and at times with the most blessed results. The Lay Preacher, or some one requested by him, should always conduct the meeting. This, to be a success, must have lively singing and short, earnest prayers. Occasionally, a short address, or a telling anecdote, might be given.

XI. *As to a Plan for the appointment of Lay Preachers.*

By way of illustrating what we mean, we will assume that an Incumbent has in his parish six preaching places and twelve Lay Preachers. For the sake of the Lay Preacher himself, and for the sake of the congregations, an arrangement must be made so that the same man shall not appear before the same people more than two Sundays in each quarter. To give a variety, the morning preacher might be at another place in the evening. A printed plan of the places in the parish, the preacher for the Sunday, the time of holding the service and when the visits of the Incumbent and his Curates shall take place, would be a very easy arrangement. The Incumbent shall make the plan, and every Lay Preacher shall be expected to take his appointment, or, in the event of his not taking it, to make suitable arrangements for it to be taken. Neglect of this, without some reasonable cause, shall involve a severe reprimand from the Incumbent, and if persisted in, a suspension of the preaching license until there be a faithful promise of amendment. The Incumbent shall have power to suspend with the sanction of the Bishop. As a natural consequence, the power to suspend the license involves the power to revoke the same.

XII. *As to Periodical Meetings of the Lay Preachers.*

Meetings of the Incumbent, Curates, and Lay Preachers should at least be once a quarter. An evening, preceded by a social tea, or an afternoon followed by the same, would be a suitable arrangement. The design of the meeting should be to have a friendly conversation on any matters affecting the promotion and prosperity of the work in hand. Reading an essay, prepared by a Lay Preacher, and a friendly criticism of the same, might be the means of imparting much valuable information. Under any circumstance, it is most desirable that there should be some definite subject before the meeting. Mere desultory talk, at such a time, is a waste of precious hours and a loss of a valuable opportunity of doing mutual good. A wise Incumbent will make the quarterly gathering of his Lay Preachers a time of much prospective pleasure. The Incumbent having sole authority in all matters relative to the working of his preaching places, the meetings shall not be for legislation, or for the voting on any question that may be mooted, or discussed. But, whilst we say there must be authority in all matters, this shall not include any alteration of well established plans in connection with lay preaching without the Bishop's consent, providing always that any Lay Preacher shall object to such an alteration. This regulation is to meet the possible contingency of a new Incumbent wishing to interfere with the regular working arrangements of his predecessor.

XIII. *As to the Lay Preacher's relationship to his Incumbent.*

Amongst some objections we have heard, is one, which to many, appears to be fraught with much possible danger, viz., Lay Preachers and their work will lessen the influence of the Incumbent. This, if of any weight, can only apply to any Incumbents and their Curates who, forgetful of their ordination vows and their "high calling." are sadly neglectful of their charge. Even then, the influence of the Lay Preacher will only be an influence (as will ever be the case) which, when connected with zeal for the salvation of souls, will always be more powerful than a life of comparative indifference in such a work. However, that there may be under any circumstance, a safe-guard for the Incumbent, it shall be understood that no Lay Preacher, through his position as such, shall have any power to interfere in parochial matters. He must in all things, appertaining to his own work, obey his Incumbent. The Incumbent's opinion, advice, or wish, shall not, under any circumstance, be put to the vote, discussed, or be called in question, only through the Bishop. This we deem to be all important. To our knowledge, "Superintendents" of "Circuits" have allowed their Local Preachers so far to interfere in matters foreign to their position as to produce much unpleasantness to both parties. The Incumbent is the recognised legal and spiritual head of his parish, and as such, he must maintain his authority. But all this may be done with a happy combination of the *suaviter in modo* with the *fortiter in re.* Let each

Incumbent, by earnest work for Christ, study to be a workman that needeth not to be ashamed, and let him be prepared to acknowledge all that is worthy in every class of his parish workers, and there will be an augmentation of influence rather than a diminution of it.

XIV. *As to the Incumbent's relationship to the congregations of his Preaching Places.*

By way of illustration, we will assume that there are six preaching places in the Parish. These have an average congregation of 250 each. The people gathered into those places have been accustomed to attend no place of worship. Whatever may be their future, possible connection with the Parish Church, or another Church of which the Preaching Place may be a nucleus, at present, they must be regarded as out-lying branches of the Parish Church, and be treated accordingly. Amongst the needs arising, in connection with the above congregations, must be reckoned, Baptism, Lord's Supper, and Churching of Women. Consequently, the Incumbent must arrange to have these attended to by himself or Curates. From this, it will be seen that the Incumbent, from the first, must have direct connection with his Preaching Places. Let then his arrangements be so made that he can periodically conduct the foregoing services. In the nature of things, it will be barely possible for the Incumbent to make his visitations at any other time than week-evenings. This may of necessity involve "Evening Communion." But as the primitive, and New Testament custom of partaking of the Lord's Supper was occasionally in the evening, a refusal to administer, because in the evening, could hardly be accounted justifiable.* A Saints' day evening could be most appropriately chosen for this sacred means of grace. Not only should the Incumbent go at proper intervals to hold the above services, but he should, at every visit, give an address or preach a sermon—short, practical, and earnest would be most commendable. Though not directly connected with his own Church, let his audience feel that they have one who loves their souls, and that their presence gives him pleasure. It is most desirable that he should occasionally bring before his hearers the wishes of the Church in reference to baptism as related to confirmation, and confirmation as related to the

---

* See Cave's Prim. Christ, Cp. 7, and Bing. Antiq. Bk. 15, Cp. 7 & 8.

Lord's Supper. Subtle, or metaphysical disquisitions on such subjects should be stringently avoided. The various teachings should be presented in a popular and practical form. Even care is essential in the use of rather antiquated and conventional phraseology. For instance, the phrase "baptismal regeneration" may be understood by intelligent church people, but to the masses it is vague, and by many of the Nonconformists it is looked upon as blasphemy, being considered to mean such a compact with the Church of God as to infallibly ensure present safety, and a future eternal life. Let all be told plainly that, as in the case of unbelieving, circumcised Jews, the very sign of the cross, may, to the enemies of Christ, be a cause for them to blaspheme (Rom. ii. 24) and, if trifled with, baptism may be the means of bringing greater punishment at the last day than will be meted out to the inhabitants of Sodom and Gomorrah. The same also of Confirmation and the Lord's Supper.

It is true that all this may bring additional labour, still souls are at stake and must not be lost, if, by being instant in season and out of season, they can be saved. But may not some Incumbents who are "in labours more abundant," lessen those labours by devoting less time to "serve tables." or by doing less purely secular work, which could be well done by lay men? Could this be done, it would give the Incumbent more time to be what his *real* vocation is—a "Cure of *Souls*." In connection with every Preaching Place, the Incumbent should strive to raise a band of praying men, who would not only be essential to the carrying on of prayer meetings at the place, but would render valuable aid in visiting the sick of the neighbourhood.

XV. *As to the Bishop's relationship to the Lay Preachers.*

Holding as the Lay Preachers do their licenses from the Bishop, it appears desirable that in the Bishop's diocesan arrangements there should be some recognition of their position and their work. We are well aware that most of the Bishops are already over-weighted with their multifarious duties. Still, would it not be possible, without much extra labour, to allow the Lay Preachers to participate, somewhat, in the privileges connected with the Bishop's periodical Visitations? However, if not feasible, the Bishop could delegate some one to act in his stead. Or, if this be found impracticable, they could at least be recognized in the Archdeacon's Visitation. A few words of welcome, or a short, timely address, would be better than no recognition of a worthy class of Christian workers. And need we remark that the adoption of something similar to the foregoing, would create a respect for lay preaching, beneficial to preachers and hearers.

As it is possible that a misunderstanding may arise between an Incumbent and his Lay Preacher, the Bishop shall have power, if requested by either party, to appoint a small committee of clergymen to hear the matter and to report their findings on the case. Acting on their report, the Bishop may give his verdict, and such verdict shall be final. Nevertheless, this verdict shall not so be interpreted as to set aside any right to be heard by the regular ecclesiastical courts as by law established, providing that, in all cases, the matter of dispute shall be included in those subjects of which the aforesaid courts may take cognizance.

XVI. *As to Itinerant Lay Preachers and Removals from Parishes.*

1. As it is possible that some Lay Preachers, with abundant leisure and means, will desire to extend their labours for their Divine Master beyond the limits of their respective parishes, they shall, with the following conditions, be allowed to do so :—(1) They shall have the consent of the Incumbent of the parish where they intend to labour. (2) It shall be deemed desirable for such consent to imply that the itinerant Lay Preacher will work under the direction of, or in co-operation with, the Incumbent. (3) The foregoing shall not be so interpreted as to mean that, in the event of an Incumbent being indifferent about the matter, the above Lay Preacher, shall, as a consequence refrain from preaching.

2. (1) In all cases of removals from one parish to another parish in the diocese, it shall be sufficient that, with the consent of his present Incumbent, the Bishop issue a fresh license, or insert in the present one the name of the parish to which the Lay Preacher is about to remove. (2) In the event of removing into a new diocese, the present license of the Lay Preacher, accompanied with a recommendation from the Incumbent, shall be deemed a sufficient reason for the Bishop of the diocese, into which he is about

to enter, to issue a fresh license. But this shall not be rendered obligatory on the part of the Bishop. Nevertheless it would be most desirable for the Bishop to issue the license, unless there be very grave reasons for refusing so to do.

XVII. *Encouragements :—*

1. *From the nature of the work which is to be done.* It has to do with saving souls and the extension of the Redeemer's kingdom amongst men. This is God's work, and is connected with the sure fulfilment of a promised outpouring of the Holy Ghost. This the truth, every Incumbent may strengthen himself for the good work, and labour hopefully in the assurance of certain success. The Lord's condition of blessing His servants' efforts is very much connected with faith—"*According* to your faith, &c." Sermons and services, special or ordinary, should always be undertaken in a lively faith that God's Holy Spirit is present to enlighten, to quicken, and to aid in man's present and eternal salvation.

2. *From what has been done outside the Church.*—No intelligent student of modern Church history can fail to notice the great religious awakening throughout the United Kingdom and America during the last century. This revival, in the main, was commenced by the Revs. J. and C. Wesley and George Whitfield, but was in a great measure carried on by Mr. Wesley's "lay helpers." And no one can fail to notice that, without those agents, well organized and incessantly at work, the movement could not have spread so widely and have taken so strong a holdfast on the sympathies and practices of the people. And, that, at the present time, the different Methodist sections throughout the world number, in their worshippers, 13,000,000, being about 2,000,000 more than the worshippers in the Church of England, must be, to a great extent, attributed to their above 60,000 Local Preachers. Such the success of a comparatively modern and voluntary system, what a stimulus ought to be given to an effort to raise Lay Preachers in the Church of England. Besides this, it is possible that some earnest Christians, who feel a wish to say something for Christ in public, but do not find an opening in the Church of England, and so are found going elsewhere, would cease to do so. It was stated at the York Convocation of 1865 that a Wesleyan Local Preacher had expressed

a wish to the speaker to join the Church of John Wesley, providing he could still continue to be a preacher. And Rev. A. Wood, of South Reston, Louth, has informed us that he is acquainted with several of the old fashioned Wesleyans who would gladly have worked for the Church of England had opportunites been afforded them, especially as Deacons or Lay Preachers.

3. *From the prospect of aiding in the supply of Clergy.* With all honour to other agencies of the Church, we cannot place preaching in an inferior position. The memories of its past trophies forbid it. Preaching—earnest, practical, faithful preaching—will ever command attention. The age is very utilitarian, and, if we mistake not, there will be an increasing demand for soul-stirring sermons. Cold, moral essays, or dry, abstract treatises on doctrine, as substitutes for Gospel-preaching, will not rouse the masses from their apathy. This the case, who better fitted ultimately to deal with men's souls than men who have had a good training as Lay Preachers? Some of the most prominent preachers amongst the Nonconformists had the best of their practical training whilst they were Local Preachers. Their going to college for two or three years did not mean a cessation of preaching. As in connection with several Theological Colleges of the Church of England, they preached on Sundays. (A good thing if some arrangement of the same kind could be made in connection with the Universities). The power of Nonconformity is chiefly in the pulpit, let not the Church of England be behind.

4. *Lastly.* Without detracting from the value of the annual "Mission," we say, get a good company of Lay Preachers, and, instead of much special effort for a few days, there will be a steady, lively action all the year round. By all means, if desired, get the Mission as usual, but have strong faith in the *continuous* "Mission" of earnest Lay Preachers. At first, difficulties may appear very great, but it will be surprising to find how smoothly the plan will work after it is fully set going. And could it be put into thorough operation, many a parish, at present comparatively barren, would have streams of the water of life, and wheresoever the waters shall come " there shall be a very great multitude of fish."

XVIII. *Objections.*
We do not lay very much stress upon this chapter. Its

being here is simply to shew that, so far as the Author has ascertained, there is not a single objection of any weight that can be brought against Lay Preaching. Anxious to ventilate the matter on a small scale, the Author secured, in connection with about forty students for the ministry, a very interesting debate of two hours on the subject. From ten to twelve spoke against the plan, but the purport of all their objections was, a creation of self-importance on the part of the Lay Preachers, or there would be a danger of getting ignorant men as preachers, or it would lessen respect for the Clergy, or it was an innovation. The answer to the first is, true religion makes man humble, and it is rather uncharitable to assert that because a man, by his gifts and graces, is raised to an important post of usefulness he will be sure to become puffed up; the reply to the second is, the examination and the license (see Chapter VIII) are a safe-guard; the reply to the third is, it is most unlikely; and the answer to the fourth is, it is true that it will be something like an innovation. Further, whilst it is an innovation, it is not the only innovation in the Church of modern times. Preaching in any place but a consecrated building is an innovation; preaching bands, as implied in the work of Mr. Aitken, are innovations; and the annual "Mission" is an innovation. And let the Divine Head of the Church be abundantly praised for such innovations—innovations whose design is to save perishing souls. But our forefathers did without such an agency. Yes, and so did they do without many things which are at the present day absolutely needful for the existence of the Church, of society, commerce, &c. Yes, granted, and granted that good Lay Preachers could do some good, still it might lead to a complete revolution in time-honoured ideas and plans. Let it be so, if the doing so shall result in rescuing scores of thousands of dying men and women. However, we fear no revolution but such as shall add glory to the Church Militant and largely increase the "innumerable company" of the Church Triumphant.

And now to God the Father, and to God the Son, and to God the Holy Ghost, Three Persons in one God, we ascribe all honour, and might, and majesty, for ever and ever. Amen.

EGGINGTON AND BROWN, PRINTERS, BIRD ST., LICHFIELD.